THOMAS & FRIENDS

Not So Secret Mission

Based on a story by **Peter Gaffney**

Adapted by **Katie Woolley**

DEAN

First published in Great Britain 2024 by DEAN, part of Farshore
An imprint of HarperCollins*Publishers*
1 London Bridge Street, London SE1 9GF
www.farshore.co.uk

HarperCollins*Publishers*
Macken House, 39/40 Mayor Street Upper,
Dublin 1, D01 C9W8, Ireland

Based on a story by Peter Gaffney
Adapted by Katie Woolley

Based on the Railway Series by The Reverend W Awdry.

ISBN 978 0 00 870679 1
Printed in China
001

A CIP catalogue record for this title is available from the British Library.

One sunny morning, Thomas rolled into Vicarstown Square. Sir Topham Hatt was rehearsing his speech for a concert that night.

"Welcome, my friends, to this musical EXTRAVAGANZA!"

Suddenly, he did an enormous jump and knocked over a streetlamp. One by one, all of the streetlamps in the square fell down with a big ***CRASH!***

"Oh, my goodness," gasped Sir Topham Hatt. "What a disaster! Everyone will be dancing in the dark, and it's all my fault! This is so embarrassing!"

"It's okay," said Thomas. "When you're with your friends, nothing can be too embarrassing. It was just an accident."

But Sir Topham Hatt felt terrible.

Thomas said he'd go and get new bulbs for the streetlamps.

"We can fix them all before anybody notices!" he said.

As he chugged away, he decided not to tell anyone what had happened.

PEEP! PEEP!

Before long, Thomas bumped into Percy.

"Hey Thomas!" said Percy. "What are you up to?"

"Oh, hey Percy," mumbled Thomas. "I'm um … doing something special for Sir Topham Hatt."

"Really?" shouted Percy. "WHAT?"

Thomas checked there was no one around. "Shh," he whispered. "I'm trying to be quiet, so Sir Topham Hatt isn't embarrassed."

Without thinking, Thomas told Percy all about the accident.

Thomas gasped and his cheeks turned red. “I wasn’t going to tell anyone! Now I’m the one who’s embarrassed!”

“Don’t worry,” said Percy. “Your mission is safe with me.”

Then Percy had an idea. “Let’s be secret agents!” he said, and the friends put on glasses and silly noses so they wouldn’t be seen!

Thomas and Percy crept towards Harwick to collect the lightbulbs.

Up ahead, Diesel was pulling Bruno along the tracks. Thomas and Percy slipped onto a sidetrack to hide from them.

"This'll be fun," whispered Thomas. Percy giggled so much he knocked over a stack of oil drums.

BANG! CRASH! CLASH!

Diesel screeched to a halt.

"Who's back there?" shouted Diesel.

Bruno could see his friends Thomas and Percy hiding, even in their disguises.

"If you're trying to hide," he called out to them, "you shouldn't make any noise!"

Thomas and Percy blushed. They felt a bit silly as they rolled onto the main track.

"What's the matter?" asked Bruno.

"I think Thomas and Percy are a little embarrassed," smiled Diesel.

"Why?" asked Bruno.

Percy blurted out the story of their secret mission for Sir Topham Hatt.

"Sounds like fun!" said Diesel. "Can we join in?"

And with that, Diesel and Bruno jumped into a nearby haystack and came out wearing straw wigs!

They all went to Harwick to get the new lightbulbs
Sir Topham Hatt needed for the concert.

As Thomas pulled crates on a flatbed, he said, "Well, that went well. No one asked why we needed lightbulbs."

The friends headed back to Vicarstown Square.

Thomas, Percy, Diesel and Bruno rolled through the countryside. Diesel zoomed ahead along the track, pulling Bruno behind him, and Thomas sped up to join the race.

As they came around a bend in the track, they spotted Kana with Annie and Clarabel. They were transporting the musicians who were going to play at the concert that night!

"STOP!" shouted Thomas as he slammed on the brakes. "We can't let them see us!"

But Thomas was going too fast, and his load of crates was too heavy!

He flew off the track and landed with a bump on the grassy hillside.

Thomas' friends rushed to help. Diesel uncoupled from Bruno and caught Thomas and the crates before they tipped over.

"Secret Agent Diesel saves the day!" said Diesel.

"Thanks," blushed Thomas. "If you hadn't been here, those bulbs would have broken."

"If we hadn't been racing, you wouldn't have gone off the tracks at all!" blushed Diesel.

"Are you embarrassed again?!" called Bruno. Thomas and Diesel nodded.

Percy joined Thomas and Diesel to help them back onto the tracks. But they were stuck in the thick grass!

“What are you all doing down there?” called a voice.

Everybody looked up to see Carly and Sandy above them.

“We were playing and got stuck,” said Thomas sheepishly.

"I wouldn't feel too bad about it," said Carly. "Sandy and I fixed the wrong bridge today."

"So, you were embarrassed too?" asked Bruno. Carly and Sandy nodded.

"It seems to me," said Bruno, "that if everybody feels embarrassed, maybe nobody needs to feel embarrassed."

"Bruno has a point," agreed Percy.

Carly and Sandy pulled the friends safely back onto the tracks.

The friends were about to head off together when Thomas' wheel gave a loud creak.

Diesel looked at his flatbed. "One of your wheels is bent," he said.

Thomas and Percy looked worried.

“What’s in those crates, anyway?” asked Sandy.

“Just some lightbulbs,” Thomas replied.

“Well, let’s split them up between us!” said Carly.

It was dark by the time everybody rolled into Vicarstown.

"I should take it from here," Thomas whispered. "Sir Topham Hatt is embarrassed about the accident, so he'd probably prefer you all didn't know."

"But we do know," said Bruno.

Sir Topham Hatt was waiting for Thomas.

"Thomas! You're here," he said. "I still feel so embarrassed, but this is easy enough to fix."

He put the first bulb into a streetlamp. "Only six more to go ..."

The light from the new bulb showed Percy waiting nearby.

"Percy!" gasped Sir Topham Hatt. "What are you doing here?"

"I'm sorry," Thomas said. "I told Percy about what happened, and he came along to help."

Then, the second lightbulb shone down on Carly and Sandy...

... and the third beamed brightly onto Bruno and Diesel.

"I guess everybody knows," sighed Sir Topham Hatt.

“You mean about you breaking those bulbs?” asked Bruno. “We know all about it … I don’t understand why everyone is embarrassed. I broke something once, too.”

“You’re right, Bruno,” agreed Sir Topham Hatt.

“But it’s hard not to feel embarrassed sometimes,” said Thomas.

“True,” said Sir Topham Hatt. “I guess there’s nothing to be embarrassed about. Especially when you’re among friends!”

Everybody laughed. Then, they worked together to fix the streetlamps just in time for the concert.

The engines gathered round to listen to Sir Topham Hatt's speech.

"Welcome, my friends, to this musical ***EXTRAVAGANZA!***" he cried.

As the music began, Percy whispered to Thomas, “I think we make good secret agents …”

Thomas smiled. “What’s our next mission?!”